The Charcoal Forest

How Fire Helps Animals and Plants

Written and illustrated
by Beth A. Peluso

Mountain Press Publishing Company
Missoula, Montana
2007

Library of Congress Cataloging-in-Publication Data

Peluso, Beth A., 1974-
  The charcoal forest : how fire helps animals and plants / written and illustrated by Beth A. Peluso.—1st ed.
     p. cm.
  ISBN 978-0-87842-532-7 (pbk. : alk. paper)
  1. Fire ecology—Rocky Mountains Region—Juvenile literature. 2. Forest ecology—Rocky Mountains Region—Juvenile literature. 3. Forest animals—Rocky Mountains Region—Juvenile literature. 4. Forest plants—Rocky Mountains Region—Juvenile literature. I. Title.
QH545.F5P45 2007
577.2'4—dc22

                                                          2007003358

Printed in Hong Kong by Mantec Production Company

Mountain Press Publishing Company
P.O. Box 2399
Missoula, MT 59806
406-728-1900

To my parents, Tom and Linda,
and my siblings, Karen and John—
see where all those family vacations led?

Acknowledgments

A round of applause for all the hardworking researchers and field biologists who find amazing answers to the simplest questions. Special thanks to Jane Kapler Smith, an ecologist at the Forest Service Rocky Mountain Research Station Fire Sciences Lab in Missoula, Montana, for help tracking down details and for reviewing the science in the book—any errors left are solely mine; Dave Dyer at the University of Montana Herbarium and Zoological Museum for many hours drawing from specimens; Dr. Diana Six at the University of Montana for insect specimens; Dr. W. G. Evans for his expertise and fantastic close-up photos of *Melanophila* beetles; Jennifer Woolf for her black-backed woodpecker photos; Bruce Byers, who sent me his research on Colorado firemoths; Don Despain, Forest Service rangeland management specialist, for information on lodgepole pines; Rick Turner, Forest Service ecologist, and Bob Gibbons, biological science technician with the Animal and Plant Health Inspection Service, for pictures of seeds; Jarod Raithel for information on elk; and to everyone who let me pepper them with questions: Sue Reel, an education specialist with the Forest Service; Amy Cilimburg, one of the authors of the "Forest Fire in the U.S. Northern Rockies" Web site; Ken Gibson, a Forest Service entomologist; Jim Habek, retired Forest Service plant ecologist; Wendy Ridenour, an ecologist; and Dr. Richard Hutto at the University of Montana.

Introduction

After a wildfire flies through a forest on burning orange wings, what happens? When the smoke drifts away, and the coals fade, many people think the blackened trees mean the forest is dead. But is it? Look closely! Insects, mammals, birds, plants, and mushrooms all call this charcoal forest home. How can any creature live here? Each bug or bird or beast or blooming thing has **adaptations**—special colors, senses, behaviors, or ways of growing—that make it possible to live in the burned zone. Some even *need* to live in burned places.

Forest fires glow across the world: North America, South America, Russia, Australia, and Africa. Different parts of North America have plants and animals adapted to fire. Forests in the Southwestern U.S. are different from West Coast forests, which are different from Southeastern forests, which in turn are different from far northern forests. This book explores one place, the northern Rocky Mountains of the United States and Canada.

What Kind of Fire Is It?

Just as there are different kinds of forest, there are different kinds of forest fires. Some fires burn close to the ground, sizzling low vegetation but not damaging many trees. These **surface fires** are often **low-severity** fires, because they don't burn hot enough to kill many plants. The opposite of these are **high-severity** fires that kill many trees. High-severity fires are what most people picture when they hear the words "forest fire": blackened trees with soot and ash everywhere. These **stand-replacing** fires are high-severity fires that burn big enough to kill whole groves of large trees. In order for the forest to recover, new seedlings sprout to replace the old, burned trees. **Crown** fires are high-severity fires that race from treetop to treetop. **Mixed-severity** fires combine pockets of low-severity fire with pockets of high-severity fire like a jigsaw puzzle. Plants and animals have adapted to different kinds of fire. Some, like the western larch, must have stand-replacing fires or they will disappear.

Low-severity fire   Mixed-severity fire   High-severity fire

Springing Back after Fire

A patch of forest usually regrows to what it looked like before a fire, but that can take hundreds of years. This book looks at what happens in burned areas the first twenty years or so after a fire. Right after a high-severity fire, the forest looks like a big charcoal drawing. If you walk through it, charred trees smudge black on your clothes and hands. But look closer: beetles feast on the dead wood left by the fire, birds dart around gobbling up beetles, and plants rush to reclaim the newly cleared ground. Those first years after a fire, plants and animals strut their stuff, showing off the most amazing adaptations. Why do some beetles fly *toward* fire? How does fire help some trees grow? This book explores those adaptations and how they work.

All of the species in this book are adapted to fire. Some species must live in burns, while others use burns if they are nearby but do just fine anywhere. You will find the following icons after each species name to indicate what type of habitat it needs:

 **Fire dependent**. Without regular fires, these species disappear.

 Fire adapted. These species include burns as one type of place they live.

 Any disturbance. These species do well in places such as roadsides and blown-down tree stands, as well as burns.

Learning More

On each page, words you may not know are in **bold**. They are usually followed by a brief definition, and there is also a glossary in the back of the book. The

"This Is the Life" section has more information about the lives of each species in *The Charcoal Forest*. The "Explore a Little More . . ." section lists other books and some Web sites about forest fires. It also includes places you can visit to see burned areas. Remember, burned areas can be dangerous. Be sure to check with the proper agency to find out if an area is safe to visit.

Scientific Names

Mountain bluebird

After the common name of each plant or animal in the "This Is the Life" section you will find its scientific name. One plant or animal may have several common names but only one scientific name. Scientific names use two Latin or Greek words to describe a **species**, a particular type of creature or plant. The first word is the **genus** and is always capitalized. Related species share the same genus name. For example, the scientific names of all three species of bluebird start with *Sialia*. The second word of a scientific name is the species name and is always lowercase. So the mountain bluebird is *Sialia currucoides*, the western bluebird is *Sialia mexicana*, and the eastern bluebird is *Sialia sialis*. You can use the genus name alone to talk about the group, but you would never use the species name by itself. Together, the genus and species provide a unique name that scientists use worldwide.

BLACK-BACKED WOODPECKER

Who needs burned trees?

The black-backed woodpecker does, for grubs and other juicy treats.

The black-backed woodpecker is an expert at living in burned woods. You will rarely find this **fire-dependent** bird outside of burns. A sooty black back makes it hard for predators to spot the bird against burned tree trunks. Males have a bright yellow cap and females have an all-black head. For two or three years after a fire, the burned trees serve as a woodpecker all-you-can-eat restaurant. Some kinds of beetles lay their eggs in trees just after a fire. The **larvae** (LAR-vee), the wormlike young of the beetles, gnaw through the wood for a year or more before becoming adults. Woodpeckers eat larvae like popcorn. A single hungry black-backed woodpecker can munch more than 13,500 beetle larvae in one year! The beetles need the burned trees for food, and the black-backed woodpecker, in turn, needs the beetle larvae for food. After the beetle grubs disappear, the woodpecker flies away to find a new charcoal forest.

Black-backed woodpeckers depend on fire.

Can you find the woodpecker in every picture?

BLACK FIRE BEETLE

Who needs burned trees?

The black fire beetle does, for a place its young can live and eat.

The black fire beetle zooms into the charcoal forest while it is still smoking. It races to be first to lay its eggs under the bark of the burned trees. The larvae feed on weakened or recently dead trees, and there are plenty after a fire. How does this insect find fires? It can sense the **infrared radiation** from the burning trees. People feel infrared as heat on their skin. To see infrared, you would have to put on a pair of night-vision goggles. A black fire beetle cannot *see* infrared either. Instead, it has two little pits on its sides that sense infrared—sometimes from over 1 mile (about 2 kilometers) away. The pits are only sensitive to a certain type of infrared radiation, the kind given off by the heat of large fires. The beetle can tell if the infrared radiation is strong or weak. It zigzags back and forth as it flies, with the infrared-sensing pits telling it if it is "hot" or "cold" on the path to the fire. Close up, this beetle's antennae can also sense temperature changes of 2 degrees Fahrenheit (just over 1 degree Celsius). That way, once it reaches the fire it can avoid sizzling in the really hot spots.

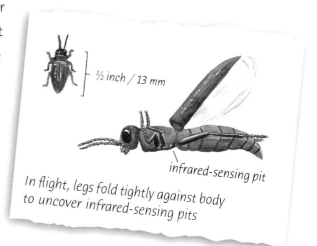

½ inch / 13 mm

infrared-sensing pit

In flight, legs fold tightly against body to uncover infrared-sensing pits

Who needs burned trees?

The lodgepole pine does, to open its cones and spread its seeds.

A fire may roast all the needles off a lodgepole pine, or even kill the tree, but the lodgepole has a backup plan. This tree grows two kinds of cones. One kind opens its scales when the seeds inside are ripe. The second kind, called a **serotinous** (suh-RAH-tuh-nus) cone, opens only after a fire. This cone may cling to the branches, waiting to release its seeds, for up to forty years! Like saving coins in a piggy bank, storing seeds for years means many seeds are ready when a fire finally comes. **Resin**, a natural glue, holds the serotinous cone closed until fire melts the resin. The sturdy cone protects the seeds from the heat. After the resin melts, the scales of the cone dry out and curl open to release the seeds. Once the seed wings covering them fall off, lodgepole seeds are black or speckled to blend in with the sooty ground after a fire. This hides them from birds or other seedeaters so they have a better chance of starting new lodgepoles in the charcoal forest.

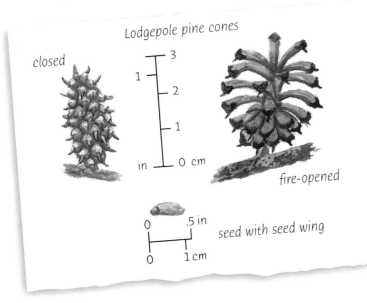

Lodgepole pine cones

closed

fire-opened

seed with seed wing

Who needs burned trees?

Black morels do, to grow fruit from the ashes.

In the year or two after a fire, crowds of black morel mushrooms pop up all over the charcoal forest. They will not be seen again in hordes until after the next fire, even if it's a century later! How can morels appear in places where no one has seen them for years? They never left. Mushrooms are like icebergs—what you see is only a small part of the whole. The mushroom you see is actually just the fruit of a fungus that grows underground. Black morels can grow unseen for decades without sprouting their mushroom fruits. The underground part of a morel is called the **mycelium** (my-SEE-lee-um) and looks like a mat of threads. To survive the cold depths of winter, the fungus grows a tough knot called a **sclerotium** (scluh-ROE-shum). In a normal spring, the sclerotium sprouts more underground mycelia, but something different happens after a fire. The burned trees provide a jackpot of extra nutrients. Add just enough springtime moisture (but not too much—black morels are picky!), and many, many mushrooms burst out of the ground in the charcoal forest.

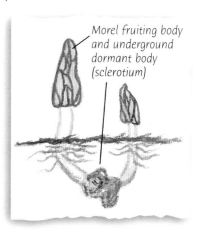

Morel fruiting body and underground dormant body (sclerotium)

PONDEROSA PINE

Who needs burned trees?

The ponderosa pine does, to keep other trees from stepping on its toes.

Like a medieval knight, a ponderosa pine wears lots of armor to survive surface fires. Very thick bark (3 inches, or 8 centimeters) provides the first line of defense. Right under the bark lies the cambium, the thin layer of the trunk where the tree grows taller and wider. If fire damages the cambium too much, the tree dies. The ponderosa pine's thick bark protects the cambium from the heat of most fires. Another ponderosa defense is self-pruning branches, which means the lower branches

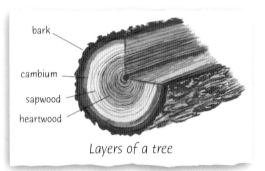

Layers of a tree

wither and drop off. This keeps the live branches high above most fires. Even the ponderosa's buds and needles have defenses against fire. Thick scales protect the buds from heat. Long needles fan out from one another, making it harder for them to catch on fire than if they were bunched tightly together. Ponderosas only a few years old can survive surface fires in the charcoal forest.

Ponderosa pine cone and seed shown at ½ actual size

two seeds fit in grooves on each scale

14

COLORADO FIREMOTH

Who needs burned trees?

The Colorado firemoth does, for bright blanketflowers to hide on as it feeds.

Would you wear bright red and yellow to hide from someone? The Colorado firemoth does! This moth spends almost its whole life on one kind of flower, the blanketflower. Blanketflowers grow best in the open spaces left by fire. When a firemoth is resting, it almost always sits so that its yellow and red parts line up with the yellow and red of the flower. This **camouflage** (CAM-uh-flahzh) helps it blend in and hide from predators. Because the moth depends on its camouflage to stay safe, it does not move very much. Unlike other moths or butterflies, it does not fly away when you come near. It's the ultimate insect couch potato!

Blanketflowers fill clearings where severe fires have killed the trees and burned the soil bare. The flowers spring up in large patches the first two years after a fire, then slowly start to disappear. By about twenty years after the fire, you won't see many blanketflowers. To find their ideal home, the firemoths have to fly in search of new burns with more flowers. They can't travel too far on their fragile wings, so they do best when there are many small burns close to each other in the charcoal forest.

WESTERN LARCH

Who needs burned trees?

The western larch does, because it grows best in bright sunbeams.

The larch has a trick that's unique among **conifers** (trees with cones). Most conifers keep the same needles for two or three years and lose them a few at a time. Not the larch. All of its needles turn sunflower yellow and drop off every autumn, so the needles are never more than five months old. Just as it

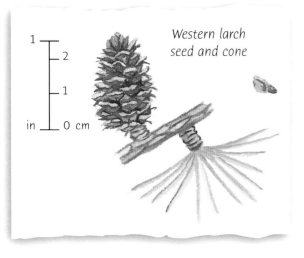

Western larch seed and cone

is harder to light a wet stick than a dry one in a campfire, the moist young larch needles do not catch fire as easily as the drier needles on other types of trees. Also, because the larch is geared to replace all its needles at once, it is easier to replace needles scorched by fire. If a fire happens in early spring, the tree may regrow new needles within one month.

The larch has other adaptations to fire. Bark up to 18 inches (45 centimeters) thick—about the width of a computer keyboard—protects mature larch trees like a fireproof jacket. These self-pruning trees keep their living branches high above most flames. Even the buds have thick, woody covers insulating them. The large trees that survive medium- to high-severity fires are right where their seeds need to be, on bare, sunny soil. Small surface fires may damage young larches, but they often recover and live for centuries in the charcoal forest.

SNOWBRUSH

Who needs burned trees?

Snowbrush does, to burst its hard seeds.

Have you ever buried a time capsule? The spring after a fire, snowbrush shrubs sprout in places they have not appeared for centuries. How? Snowbrush seeds have extremely hard, waterproof shells. These miniature vaults keep the seed inside alive but **dormant**, or inactive, sometimes for hundreds of years! When a low- or medium-severity fire heats the seed in the ground to between 176 and 204 degrees Fahrenheit (80 to 96 degrees Celsius), the scar where the seed was attached to its parent plant cracks open. Water trickles inside and the seedling finally starts to uncurl. Fire burns away piles of leaves and twigs that buried the seeds over the years, giving the emerging seedlings a chance to reach the surface.

Snowbrush bushes have another trick for surviving fire. When fire kills its leaves and branches, the plant regrows from the deep roots left behind. In the first three years after a fire, a snowbrush shrub may reach 3 to 5 feet (1 to 1.5 meters) high. In some places, snowbrush rules the charcoal forest until trees grow tall enough to block the sunlight.

Snowbrush fruit

Snowbrush seed sprouting

Snowbrush seed actual size

0 1 2 cm   1 in

CLARK'S NUTCRACKER

Who needs burned trees?

The Clark's nutcracker does, for places to store pine seeds.

The Clark's nutcracker swoops through high mountain forests searching for its favorite food, whitebark pine seeds. The pine and the nutcracker have a great partnership: the tree provides seeds the bird eats, and the bird carries the seeds to open, sunny spaces—often in burns—where whitebark pines grow best. Nutcrackers depend on whitebark pine (and a few other pines) that depend on fire.

Can you imagine carrying your groceries under your tongue? The Clark's nutcracker has a special pouch under its tongue to carry seeds—up to one hundred at once! The nutcracker's throat bulges when it holds a full load of seeds. This bird spends most of the summer and fall breaking open pinecones and **caching** (CASH-ing), or storing, seeds for the winter. Sometimes it flies up to 7 miles (11 kilometers) from where it gathered the seeds, caching them in piles of up to fifteen seeds, usually in burned areas. One bird can stash between 35,000 and 98,000 seeds a year! The nutcracker remembers where the piles are compared to nearby rocks or logs. It can return to a cache nine months later, poke around with its beak, and unearth a meal. The Clark's nutcracker usually buries two to three times as many seeds as it needs for the winter. The seeds it does not eat can grow into new whitebark pines in the charcoal forest.

WHITEBARK PINE

Who needs burned trees?

The whitebark pine does, to keep its growing space open and neat.

Whitebark pine seedlings need open, sunny places. This high-elevation pine is a **pioneer species**, one of the first trees to sprout in newly burned ground where fire has cleared the way. Whitebark pines survive surface fires better than competing fir and spruce trees do. Without surface fires, firs and spruces eventually block out the sunlight. No new whitebark pines can take root under the shady branches. With fire, whitebark pine seedlings can grow on the sunny mountainsides of the charcoal forest.

Unlike most pines, whitebark pines have heavy seeds that do not float on the wind. So how do they travel? They taste good! The Clark's nutcracker likes to eat them so much it carries the seeds away and buries them for later, usually in burned areas. Some of the seeds that the bird—or grizzly bear or squirrel—doesn't snack on sprout into seedlings. Whitebark pines make the seeds easy for nutcrackers to find. The branches curve upward, with cones held high. The cones stay closed, even when the seeds are ripe. That way, the nutcrackers don't have to waste time looking for seeds scattered on the ground.

Whitebark pine cone and seed

24

HORNTAIL WASP

Who needs burned trees?

The horntail wasp does, for trees where its young can munch their favorite treat.

Horntail wasp larvae are picky eaters: they only eat a certain kind of fungus that grows in dead or dying wood. Trees killed or wounded by fire make perfect horntail nurseries. The female horntail plants some of the fungus when she lays her eggs. How? Female horntails have long, thin **ovipositors** (tubes for laying eggs). The ovipositor folds against the female's body like a pocketknife and looks like a huge stinger. (Luckily, horntails cannot sting!) The female drills into wood with her ovipositor to lay her eggs inside. Organs in the ovipositor sense moisture in the wood. Only injured or dying trees have the right amount of moisture. Two pouches at the base of the ovipositor hold fungus **spores** (tiny, seedlike structures that start a new fungus). When the female lays an egg, spores attach to it.

The fungus starts growing in the tree. When the egg hatches, the larva's first breakfast is ready to go! The fungus also softens the wood so the larva can tunnel through it. As the larva digs into the tree, the fungus spreads with it. After two or three years, when the larva is large enough, it changes into an adult, gnaws its way out, and flies away into the charcoal forest.

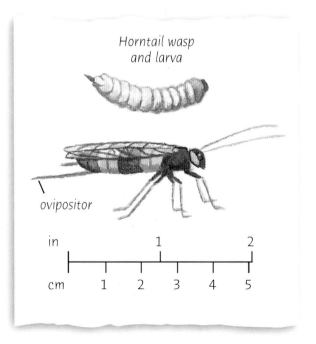

Horntail wasp and larva

ovipositor

26

QUAKING ASPEN

Who needs burned trees?

The quaking aspen does, for sunlight to grow new sprouts and leaves.

Many of the quaking aspen groves in the Rockies are **clones**, "identical twin" trees sprouting from a single root system. Sometimes thousands of trees share the same roots. Quaking aspen clones can live several thousand years! How can a plant live so long? Fire. Without fire, aspen trees grow old and are easily damaged by insects or fungi. New trees need bright sunlight—even the flickering shade of aspen leaves is too dark. Hot flames sweep away old trees, allowing light to reach the ground. After a fire, new shoots use the food stored in the clone's root system to spring up faster than conifers. Aspen roots have buds just waiting for a good burn. Living branch buds and leaves produce a **hormone**, or chemical, that prevents the root buds from growing. When fire burns off the leaves and branch buds, they cannot produce the hormone. Soon a whole forest of tiny aspens springs up from ancient roots in the charcoal forest. Ten years after a fire, a new aspen grove dances in the breeze.

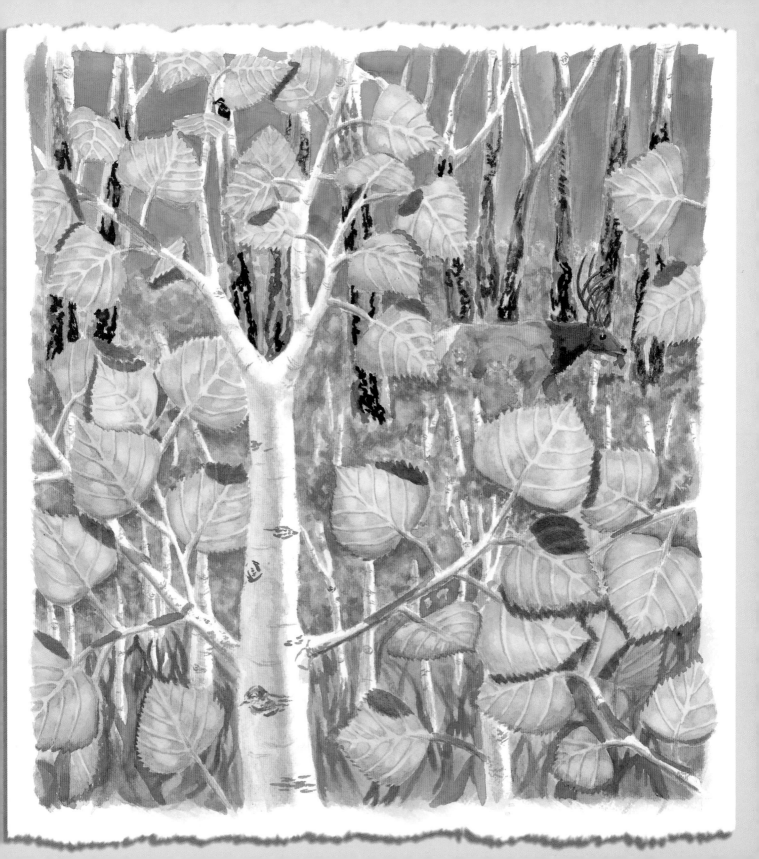

DEER MOUSE

Who needs burned trees?

The deer mouse does, for open space to scramble on tiny feet.

The deer mouse feasts in the spaces cleared by a fire. The deer mouse is **nocturnal** (active at night), so it doesn't need thick plants to hide in. This small rodent is an **omnivore**, so, like a miniature grizzly bear, it eats everything: seeds, nuts, berries, fungi, and insects. If you were a tiny beetle, a deer mouse would be a very scary predator! Fire burns away dead leaves on the ground, exposing hidden seeds, like those from snowbrush bushes. Other plants, such as lodgepole pines, release seeds in response to fire. A single mouse can gobble up hundreds of seeds in one night.

About two weeks after a fire, deer mice begin moving into a burned area. Sometimes a few early mice show up before the coals cool off. Often, deer mice are the first mammals to brave the scorched ground. The light, fluffy ash can be difficult for short mouse legs, so sometimes they wait until rain packs down the ash. Parents chase youngsters away when they are old enough to live on their own. Many of the mice that move into the charcoal forest are searching for their first home away from Mom and Dad. Three or four years after a fire, most deer mice leave because the plant litter on the ground piles up too high, making it hard for the mice to find food or scamper around.

30

Who needs burned trees?

The huckleberry bush does, for new branches to grow fat, sweet berries.

Without fire, huckleberry bushes gradually disappear. Without enough light, the bush can't grow and berries ripen weeks late. Without the right amount of shade, berries have tough skins and are not very juicy. Surface fires clear away shrubs and young trees that block the bush's sun. Taller trees that survive the fire partly shade the huckleberries, giving them just the right amount of dappled light.

Only an intense fire can kill a tough huckleberry bush. The leathery leaves do not burst into flame easily, just as it is much harder to burn a piece of leather than a piece of paper. Huckleberries only ignite after wood or leaf litter burning near them has heated and dried out the leaves. A high-severity fire may burn deep enough to kill the **rhizomes** (RYE-zomes), or underground stems, so the bushes won't grow back. But when a low- or medium-severity fire burns away old huckleberry branches, crowds of new stems replace them in about five years, making the patch denser. The new stems grow from buds at the bottom of the charred old stems or from the rhizomes. Denser huckleberry patches mean more huckleberries! But you may have to wait anywhere from five to twenty years for the plants to recover enough for lots of berries in the charcoal forest.

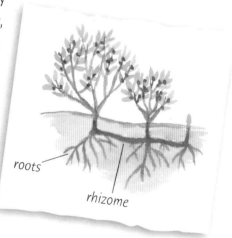

roots

rhizome

Who needs burned trees?

The elk does, for green meadows where it feeds.

Burned areas are one big salad bar for an elk. Shrubs such as snowbrush and huckleberry, along with young aspen, help the elk survive harsh mountain winters. In spring and summer, grasses and plants, such as fireweed, grow densely in the ashy, vitamin-rich soil. Female elk need lots of vitamins in spring while nursing their calves, so they often eat in these new fields.

Elk need burns for more than food. Mixed-severity fires and burns of different ages can create a **mosaic** landscape, a patchwork quilt of everything from dense forest to open meadows. On a hot summer day, elk cool off in the shade of trees or shrubs along meadow edges. **Snags**, standing dead trees, in burned areas help elk hide from predators. In winter, elk use different ages of burns depending on the snow. For about ten years after a fire, grass and soft-stemmed plants cover the ground. When snow lies shallow and soft, elk keep to grassy meadows. Shrubs replace grasses, with the shrubs thickest about twenty years after a fire. When snow is belly deep in the meadows, or covered with an icy crust, elk trudge to shrubby places with less snow, where they munch on bushes. After about twenty years, trees take over, providing a place where elk retreat if the snow is very deep. By moving between old and new burned areas, elk use the charcoal forest as a home for all seasons.

34

Who needs burned trees?

The mountain bluebird does, for a safe place to build its nest.

Mountain bluebird pairs raise their chicks in holes in trees. But if a bluebird tried to drill into a tree, it would knock itself silly. Where does the nest cavity come from? Mountain bluebirds shop around for empty woodpecker holes in burned areas. After a fire, many kinds of woodpeckers move into the charcoal forest to eat the bonanza of insect larvae. They carve nest holes in trees, then abandon the holes when their chicks leave the nest. A male bluebird finds several promising old woodpecker holes when he arrives in spring. When the female returns, he flutters around and chirps at each hole, trying to show her how great it is. The female chooses a hole and builds a nest inside. Mountain bluebirds start nesting in April. A warm, dry woodpecker hole protects the babies from spring snowstorms.

The mountain bluebird perches on low branches or hovers while on the prowl for insects. It prefers to hunt on bare ground or where the plants are very short, no higher than a thick carpet. Not only can the bluebird see the food better in open places, it can also watch for predators that want to eat it. The first few years after a fire, the charcoal forest provides bluebirds with a perfect blend of open spaces and good perches.

GRIZZLY BEAR

Who needs burned trees?

The grizzly bear does, for huckleberries and other good things to eat.

What would you eat if you could only have food for four months of the year? Everything! The grizzly bear **hibernates**, or sleeps, from about October through May. When it wakes up in spring, this omnivore is an eating machine. Although its 4-inch claws and huge teeth look like they're made just for tearing into meat, a grizzly's menu also includes plant shoots and roots—which it digs up with its claws—conifer seeds, insects, and berries. In different seasons, burns of different ages hold the variety of foods a grizzly needs to survive the long nap. The bear snuffles around a recent burn for animals killed in the fire. It rips open burned logs for ants and insect larvae. In spring and early summer, the grizzly munches on juicy plants and morel mushrooms in burns a few years old. In late summer, the bear searches for ripe huckleberries on older burns. At higher elevations, the grizzly adds whitebark pine seeds to its snack list. When it can find small mammals, such as deer mice or ground squirrels, it eats them, too. Everything in the charcoal forest is tasty to a grizzly!

LUNG LIVERWORT 🔥

Who needs burned trees?

Lung liverwort does, because it needs space free from trees.

You can't have a party with one person, right? One lung liverwort plant needs other lung liverworts to keep it company. As soon as a tiny lung liverwort spore lands on the scene of a burn, the plant begins spreading. Places where the bare soil left by a severe fire is slightly moist provide perfect growing spots. A single liverwort quickly dries out in the sun, but a bunch of plants with their leaves packed together hold lots of water. For the first three years after a fire, clumps of lung liverwort shade out small plants. The flat, low-lying leaves of a liverwort cannot compete with taller plants, so eventually other, taller plants take over.

Lung liverworts have not one, not two, but three ways of spreading so they can fill space quickly. First, leaves that have broken off can grow into another plant. Second, lung liverwort produces special stems that look like tiny wine glasses for grasshoppers. Each cup holds little Frisbees of a dozen or so cells, called **gemmae** (JEM-ee), that come from a single parent liverwort. When rain splashes into the cup, it washes the gemmae out. They start new plants right next door. The third way involves spores that develop inside jellyfish-shaped capsules on stalks. When the capsules release the tiny spores, the spores can travel long distances on the wind to colonize a new part of the charcoal forest.

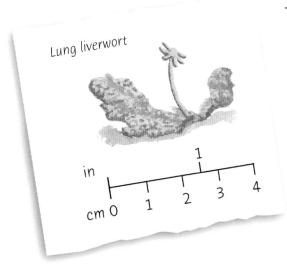

Lung liverwort

in

1

cm 0   1   2   3   4

40

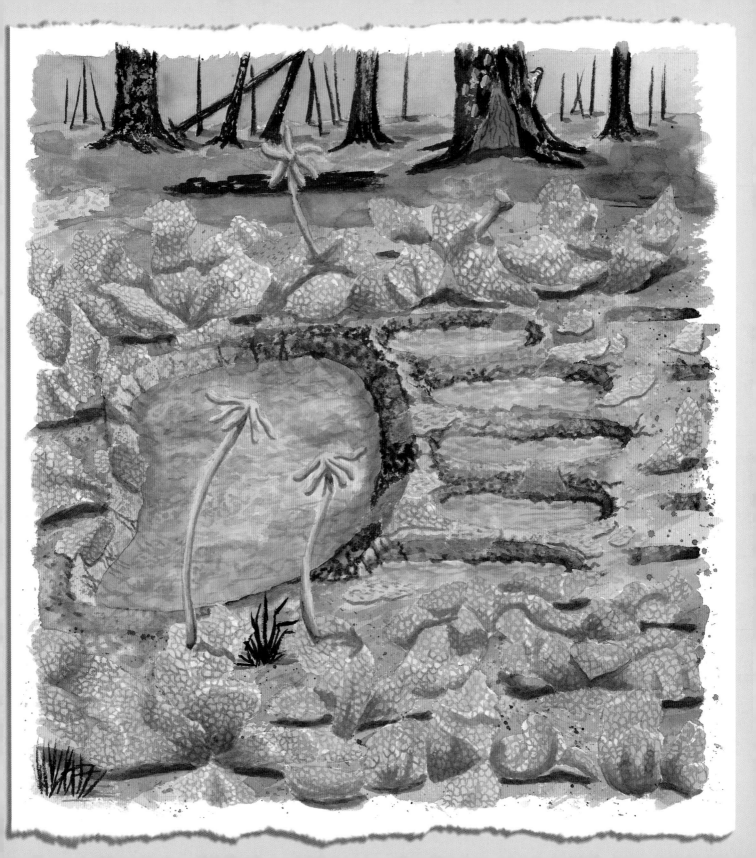

FIRE MOSS

Who needs burned trees?

Fire moss does, to burn old plants and wipe the soil clean.

Roll out the moss carpet, the fire is over! Fire moss grows anywhere with bare, compacted soil, such as the cracks in a sidewalk or next to a stream—or on the bare earth after a fire. The moss needs bright sunlight, so an intense fire that chars everything helps the moss. This pioneer plant holds the dirt floor of the forest in place. Otherwise, water and wind would sweep the soil away. Clumps of fire moss may rule parts of the burn for anywhere from a few years to twenty years after a fire.

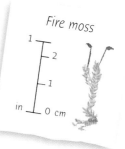

Fire moss

Flames burn fire moss to a crisp. So how do new plants arrive at a burn? Air express. Mosses have very simple seedlike spores, tiny enough to float on the wind like specks of dust. Each fire moss plant releases millions of spores. Spores can last a long time—sometimes up to fifteen years. When one lands on a burn, it immediately sends out green threads. Once it has a good hold on the ground, each thread, called a **protonema** (pro-tuh-NEE-muh), grows into a leafy moss that carpets the charcoal forest.

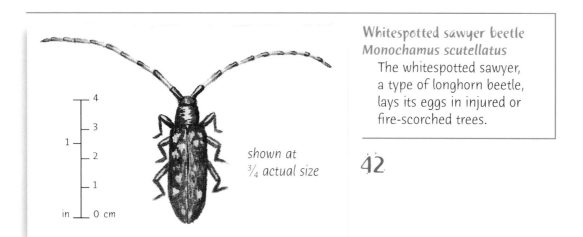

shown at
¾ actual size

Whitespotted sawyer beetle
Monochamus scutellatus
The whitespotted sawyer, a type of longhorn beetle, lays its eggs in injured or fire-scorched trees.

42

FIREWEED

Who needs burned trees?

Fireweed does, for sunny spots to stretch its leaves.

Fireweed finds the bare soil and bright sunlight it needs in burned places. Brilliant fields of fireweed flowers surround charred trees a year or two after a fire.

How did they get there? Fireweed seeds have fluffy white parachutes that float on the slightest wind. A strong breeze can carry fireweed seeds over 100 miles (161 kilometers). Humidity causes the parachutes to close a little, so the seed drifts to the ground. This gives the seed a better chance of touching down in a moist site where it can take root. Most fireweed seeds (one plant can produce 80,000 seeds!) cannot grow where they land. That is why the plants produce so many seeds. A few lucky ones will find a fire zone with lots of light and start a new field of flowers in the charcoal forest.

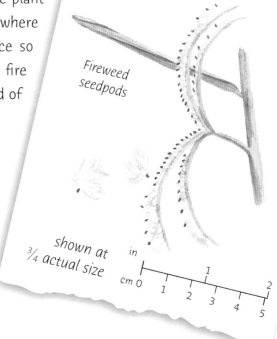

Fireweed seedpods

shown at ¾ actual size

in

cm 0   1   2   3   4   5

1   2

This Is the Life

Below is more information about the lives of the plants and animals in *The Charcoal Forest*. They are listed in alphabetical order.

Big Huckleberry
Vaccinium membranaceum

Too much sun turns huckleberry leaves red. For huckleberries, this is like putting on sunglasses. The red pigment protects the part of the leaves with **chlorophyll**, the green pigment plants use to create food. Grizzly bears love to munch on huckleberries, but they will also snack on the leaves.

Black-backed Woodpecker
Picoides arcticus

From the time it hatches, a black-backed woodpecker spends almost its whole life in the charcoal forest. As a nestling (before it can fly), it stays in a nest cavity its parents hollowed out in a tree. These woodpeckers like to nest where there are lots of burned trees. Usually, the hole is in a small or medium-sized snag, a standing dead tree. When they can fly, the young birds shadow their parents for a summer, climbing trees and practicing how to peck just like Mom and Dad. They feast on bark beetle and wood-boring beetle larvae found in dead trees, but they will also snack on berries, acorns, ants, and spiders. Black-backed woodpeckers often search for beetles by tearing chunks of bark off a tree. If you watch closely, you will see a black-backed woodpecker close its eyes when it pecks hard to keep out flying wood chips. If you see quarter-sized patches of bark missing on a burned tree, it could be where a black-backed woodpecker had dinner.

Black Fire Beetle
Melanophila acuminata

The larvae of these beetles have large, flat heads, so they are often called flat-headed borers. When a larva hatches, it chews its way into the wood of the tree. For a year or more it gnaws tunnels until it grows large enough to change into an adult. Sometimes you can find a log with the beetles' tunnels twisting across it. (The log in the snowbrush painting on page 21 has beetle tunnels on it.)

Black Morels
Morchella angusticeps,
Morchella conica,
Morchella elata

Black morels raise their heads out of the ground in early spring, just a few weeks after the snow melts. (Mushroom fans call the bump in the ground made by a growing mushroom a "mushrump.") In a few weeks, the pale young mushrooms grow into adults with dark ridges. Morels can grow over 10 inches (25 centimeters) tall. They release all their spores at once. If you touch or blow on a morel when its spores are ready, they will all fly out in a little puff of "smoke." Deer, elk, squirrels, and chipmunks nibble on black morels whenever they can.

Clark's Nutcracker
Nucifraga columbiana

Nutcrackers hatch when winter still howls through the mountains in January or February. The family travels together through spring and summer, feasting on seeds the parents gathered the year before. By fall, when the next crop of pine seeds ripens, the young birds know how to collect and hide their own seeds. Aside from their main dish of whitebark pine seeds, nutcrackers will eat nearly anything: insects, spiders, dead animals, eggs, other birds, chipmunks, and toads.

Colorado Firemoth
Schinia masoni
Not all moths flutter around in the moonlight. Firemoths are **diurnal**, which means that they fly and feed during the day. Firemoths are only found in one small part of the United States—a narrow strip of the Rocky Mountains in Colorado and a sliver of southern Wyoming. Adult moths drink the sweet nectar of the blanketflower (*Gaillardia aristata*). They lay their eggs in the center of the blossom. The larvae hatch and eat the flower and the developing seeds. The only time a firemoth lives away from home is while it is changing into an adult in the soil.

Deer Mouse
Peromyscus maniculatus
If fire catches up to a deer mouse, the mouse may escape by hiding in an underground burrow or by leaving the area. These rodents have short lives—many only live for 1 year. In winter, deer mice eat aspen bark buried under the snow. Sometimes they use fallen logs as mouse highways.

Elk
Cervus canadensis
Fires rarely harm elk. A few very young calves may have trouble escaping flames, but most adults wander out of the way. During the huge Yellowstone fires of 1988, elk often grazed in meadows next to blazing trees without twitching an ear. Elk love to eat every part of young aspens, from tender leaves and twigs to bark.

Elk live for 10 to 12 years. Male elk can weigh in at 700 pounds (320 kilos), while females are around 500 pounds (225 kilos). During mating season, male elk "bugle" from dusk to dawn. This eerie sound starts low and slides up to a high wail, ending in grunting sounds. The bugle attracts female elk and warns other males away.

Fire Moss
Ceratodon purpureus
Mosses are primitive plants. In more complex plants, only a certain kind of cell carries water through the plant. In mosses, all cells can soak up water like a sponge. When they can soak up water, fire moss plants are green and spread out. When water is scarce, the leaves curl up and dry out. A complex plant would die, but a moss enters a type of suspended animation. It does not grow, but remains alive.

A brown stalk with a capsule where spores form grows from the leafy part of the moss. Fire moss often keeps company with fireweed, another pioneer species.

Fireweed
Epilobium angustifolium
Fireweed grows best in soil where fire has burned away all the dead leaves. Once a few plants take hold in a clearing, they colonize the whole area. Underground stems called rhizomes spread out and grow new stalks. A rhizome from 1 plant can reach up to 20 feet (about 6 meters) long. If a surface fire crisps all the stems and leaves, fireweed regrows from the rhizomes and may bloom again in a month.

Fireweed shoots are packed with protein and vitamins. Grizzly bears, elk, mule deer, and bighorn sheep enjoy summer fireweed salads. The tall sprays of flowers take all summer to bloom from the bottom up. Hummingbirds, bees, and butterflies drink the flower nectar. In autumn, fireweed seedpods burst open and the seeds float away on their fluffy parachutes. Chipmunks sometimes munch on the crunchy seeds.

Grizzly Bear
Ursus arctos horribilis
Fires kill very few grizzlies. When flames crackle through a grizzly's home, most bears leave only for a short time. Some even stay nearby, just beyond the fire. As soon as the fire sputters out, the grizzlies return, searching for barbecued dinners and other delicacies.

Grizzly bears are not very good hunters, so most of their prey are small rodents or very young or weak larger animals. Grizzlies have to fatten up at the end of the summer to prepare for their long winter sleep.

They sometimes pack on 400 pounds (180 kilos) of winter weight! These large bears live anywhere from 15 to 35 years. Females usually have their first cubs between 5 and 8 years old. Only very young grizzlies are light enough to climb trees.

Horntail Wasp
Sirex species and *Urocerus* species

Female horntails lay 300 to 400 eggs, 1 at a time. The larvae do not chew their food; they spit on it—their saliva breaks down the fungus that they feed on so they can eat it. After 2 or 3 years, when they are big enough, they spend 5 or 6 weeks changing into winged adults. The new adults gnaw their way out of the wood, leaving a round hole the size of your pinky fingertip. Right before she breaks into the outside world, the female twists and squirms in the fungus to make sure she carries some for her own eggs. Males wriggle free and fly directly to the treetops. Females join them a week or so later to mate. Adult horntails drink flower nectar and water.

Lodgepole Pine
Pinus contorta latifolia

Although fire kills some lodgepoles, it helps them in the long term. Fires leave sunny, open spots perfect for lodgepole seedlings. The slender pines live an average of 200 years, although some groves in Yellowstone are over 350 years old. Lodgepoles begin growing cones very young, about 5 or 10 years old. At first, they only grow regular cones. When they reach 20 to 30 years old, they can start growing serotinous cones. In places where fire occurs often, lodgepoles have mostly serotinous cones. In places with fewer fires, the trees have mostly non-serotinous cones. The resin on the serotinous cones melts at about 115 degrees Fahrenheit (46 degrees Celsius). A high-severity fire can turn a lodgepole's needles and very small twigs to ash, and melt the resin, in under 30 seconds. After the fire, the cones can open in as short as half an hour.

Lung Liverwort
Marchantia polymorpha

"Wort" is an old English word for "plant." The name "liverwort" comes from the bumpy surface of the lobed leaves, which people thought looked like a liver. Liverworts are primitive plants, like mosses. Liverwort leaves are often only a single cell thick. The parts of the plant that produce spores spring up as soon as the snow melts in spring.

Mountain Bluebird
Sialia currucoides

Although they are small, bluebirds are strong enough to survive temperatures of 10 degrees Fahrenheit (-12 degrees Celsius). Baby bluebirds double their weight 2 or 3 times the first week after they hatch. Just 20 days after struggling out of their shells, they can fly clumsily away from the nest. Mountain bluebird families spend the summer together, sometimes flocking with other families. In the fall large flocks of bluebirds migrate south for the winter.

Ponderosa pine
Pinus ponderosa

A healthy ponderosa forest has large, widely spaced trees because frequent surface and mixed-severity fires clear away brush and less fire-resistant tree species. Ponderosa seedlings need bright sunlight and are usually one of the first trees to sprout after fire. Ponderosas are one of the giants of the Rocky Mountain forests. The top branches can tower 150 feet (46 meters) over the forest floor. Many ponderosas live for 300 or 400 years, and some as long as 700 years. Ponderosas take several years to produce a crop of seeds. If you lean in close, you may catch a whiff of vanilla from the bark.

Quaking Aspen
Populus tremuloides

Sometimes fires sputter out when they reach an aspen grove because of the moist soil, but even a surface fire that stays lit will kill young trees and damage larger ones. A medium-severity fire kills all but the largest trees.

When you see a creek lined with golden aspens in autumn, you probably see a clone. All the trees in a clone grow new leaves in spring and lose them in the fall at the same time. Although the roots may live for thousands of years, 150 years is old for individual aspen trunks. Quaking aspens flower for the first time when they are only 2 or 3 years old. One tree can release over 1 million seeds each year. These fragile seeds only last a few weeks, so they need to land in a perfect spot. A sunny place with bare soil and no competing plants provides a good home for baby aspens. Seedlings do not often survive in the dry Rocky Mountains, but after the large Yellowstone fires of 1988, aspen seedlings colonized the charcoal black soils of many burns.

The silvery green bark on an aspen can create food for the plant from sunlight, water, and carbon dioxide just like the leaves do. The white powder on some bark is the tree's natural sunscreen to protect its pale skin.

Snowbrush
Ceanothus velutinus

Often you can smell the strong, cinnamon odor of snowbrush leaves before you see the plant. Clusters of tiny, white snowbrush flowers open in late spring. By the end of the summer they have changed into 3-lobed seedpods. When the seeds are ripe, the pods pop, flinging seeds far and wide. Many small mammals, such as chipmunks and deer mice, munch on the seeds. Mule deer and sometimes elk like to eat snowbrush leaves, which can be an important food for these animals in the winter. Birds like to nest in the dense branches.

Western Larch
Larix occidentalis

Larches can reach up to 180 feet (55 meters) tall, with trunks stretching 6 feet (2 meters) wide. Some trees live for over 900 years. Their roots reach deep underground, anchoring the trees against strong mountain winds. Larch seedlings, if they have a sunny open burn to grow in, shoot up faster than everything except lodgepole pines.

Whitebark Pine
Pinus albicaulis

Clark's nutcrackers bury several seeds together, so you often find whitebark pines growing together in clumps. Sometimes the trees grow so close together their trunks touch or even fuse into one giant trunk. These slow-growing pines can live for hundreds, sometimes over 1,000, years. High in the mountains where whitebarks live, most of the water comes from melting snow in the spring. If it's on a ridge, the spreading branches of a whitebark pine block the wind, building snowdrifts. In the spring, the piles of snow take a long time to melt, providing water for a longer time than in places without whitebark pines.

Explore a Little More . . .

BOOKS

The Book of Fire, 2nd ed. William H. Cottrell, Jr. Missoula, MT: Mountain Press, 2004.
> The first half of the book discusses how fire works; the second half focuses on how forest fires burn.

Fire: Friend or Foe? Dorothy Hinshaw Patent. New York: Clarion Books, 1998.
> Covers a wide range of forest types, including ponderosa, redwood, and rain forest.

A Forest Is Reborn. James R. Newton. New York: Thomas Y. Crowell, 1982.
> Good illustrations of the different stages of regrowth after fire.

Summer of Fire: Yellowstone 1988. Patricia Lauber. New York: Orchard Books, 1991.
> A vivid description of the fires and how plants recovered afterward. Includes many photos.

Yellowstone Fires: Flames and Rebirth. Dorothy Hinshaw Patent. New York: Holiday House, 1990.
> Good photos.

WEB SITES

Lolo National Forest, Fire Education, "Life After a Fire" www.fs.fed.us/r1/lolo/resources-natural/wildlife/after-fire/index.htm
> Good background fire information. Click on pictures of mountain scenes to learn about different forest types and the animals that live in them.

"Forest Fire in the U.S. Northern Rockies: A Primer" www.northernrockiesfire.org
> Lots of information about many different topics, from fire history to forest types.

PLACES TO VISIT

Always remember to ask the information or visitor center staff if a burned area is safe to hike in before exploring!

Banff National Park, Alberta, Canada

Box 900
Banff, AB T1L 1K2
Canada
403-762-1550
www.banff.vrc@pc.gc.ca
www.pc.gc.ca/pn-np/ab/banff
> Go to "Park Management" and then "Fire and Vegetation" for fire information and to learn how the park managers use fire as a tool to keep the forest healthy. The "Where's the Fire? A Roadside Guide" tells where you can go in the park to see sites where past fires burned.

> NOTE: The National Parks of Canada Web site has information about fire and how the parks use it as a management tool at www.pc.gc.ca/progs/np-pn/eco/eco5_E.asp#a2.

Glacier National Park, Montana

Park Headquarters
P.O. Box 128
West Glacier, MT 59936
406-888-7800
www.nps.gov/glac
> As of January 2007, the park was updating its Web site. The old fire Web site has video clips of past fires:
> www.nps.gov/archive/glac/resources/fire2003/2003gallery.htm

Lolo National Forest, Western Montana

This national forest offers field trips about fire in the Lolo National Forest for kids. Contact wildlife interpretive specialist Sue Reel at 406-329-3831 or sreel@fs.fed.us.

Montana Natural History Center, Missoula, Montana

120 Hickory St.
Missoula, MT 59801
406-327-0405
info@MontanaNaturalist.org
www.montananaturalist.org

There is a small exhibit here on fire effects; post-fire ecology; and the birds, bugs, and trees that are adapted to living with fire.

Rocky Mountain National Park, Colorado

1000 Highway 36
Estes Park, CO 80517
970-586-1206
www.nps.gov/romo
www.nps.gov/romo/naturescience/fire.htm

Brief Web page on the role of fire and fire management, including some good photos.

Waterton National Park, Alberta, Canada

Box 200
Waterton Park, AB T0K 2M0
Canada
403-859-2224
waterton.info@pc.gc.ca
www.pc.gc.ca/pn-np/ab/waterton

Fire information: Click on "Natural Wonders & Cultural Treasures," then "Fire, Flood and Avalanche."

Yellowstone National Park, Idaho, Montana, and Wyoming

Information Office
P.O. Box 168
Yellowstone National Park, WY 82190-0168
307-344-7381
yell_visitor_services@nps.gov
www.nps.gov/yell/naturescience/fire.htm.

Lots of fire facts, especially about the large 1988 fires. If you click on the link to the "Main Wildland Fire Section" there is a map of currently burning fires during fire season (late summer through autumn). At the Grant Village Visitor Center you can watch a video of the 1988 fires.

Yoho National Park, British Columbia, Canada

P.O. Box 99
Field, BC V0A 1G0
Canada
250-343-6783
yoho.info@pc.gc.ca
www.pc.gc.ca/pn-np/bc/yoho

Click on "Natural Wonders & Cultural Treasures" for good information on the role of fire in this ecosystem, as well as a glossary of fire terms.

FOR TEACHERS

"Fire Effects Information System"
www.fs.fed.us/database/feis/

This Forest Service database contains a wealth of scientific information about how fire affects plants, animals, and ecosystems. It also has an extensive glossary.

Educational Trunks

The Montana Natural History Center has a long list of educational trunks on a wide range of topics for the northern Rockies. See www.montananaturalist.org.

FIREWORKS TRUNK: Grades 1–12, available in multiple states. The curriculum focuses on ponderosa, whitebark, and lodgepole pine forests.

Glossary

adaptation. In plants and animals, a change in structure or behavior over a long period of time that allows the species to survive better in a particular habitat.

cache. To store something, such as food, for future use.

cambium. The layer of a tree that grows, located between the bark and the wood. The yearly growth of the cambium creates the rings in a tree trunk. The cambium also forms scars around injuries.

camouflage. Coloring or body shape that helps an animal blend into its surroundings.

chlorophyll. The green pigment in plant leaves that enables the plant to make energy from sunlight, water, and carbon dioxide gas.

clone. A genetic duplicate; a plant or animal that has grown from a single parent, as in aspens.

conifer. Trees that bear their seeds in cones, such as pines and larches.

crown fire. A quick-moving, usually high-severity fire that travels from treetop to treetop.

disturbance. A place where something has changed the forest, usually by removing trees or moving the soil; natural examples include fire, flood, and strong winds.

diurnal. Describes an animal that is active during the day and rests at night.

dormant. Describes a state of "suspended animation" or deep rest in which a plant's or animal's system drastically slows down.

fire adapted. Said of species that do well in burned areas but also live in other types of habitat.

fire dependent. Said of species that need the habitat produced by fire to survive, such as black-backed woodpeckers.

gemma (plural gemmae). In liverworts, a small disk of cells released by a single parent plant that grows into a new plant.

genus. A group of related species. In the scientific name of a species, the first word of the name. For example, *Pinus* is the genus name of several species of pines: ponderosa pine (*Pinus ponderosa*), whitebark pine (*Pinus albicaulis*), and lodgepole pine (*Pinus contorta*).

hibernate. What animals such as bears do, falling into an extremely deep sleep for the winter. The heartbeat slows down and the animal lives off fat stored in its body.

high-severity fire. A fire that burns very hot, killing large trees. See **stand-replacing fire** and **crown fire**.

hormone. A chemical that controls changes in a plant or animal.

infrared radiation. A type of energy like light, except that it is not visible to the human eye. Humans sense it as heat. "Infra" means "below." The wavelength of infrared radiation is closest to the wavelength of visible red light.

larva (plural larvae). The wormlike stage of an insect's life, after it hatches from the egg.

low-severity fire. A fire that burns low to the ground, charring plants and shrubs. This fire type is common in ponderosa pine forests. See also **surface fire**.

mixed-severity fire. A fire that burns in a patchwork of low and high severities—in some parts everything burns, and in others many trees survive.

mosaic. A landscape with patches in different stages of regrowth or different fire types. For example, a new burn near a twenty-year-old burn next to a one-hundred-year-old burn.

mycelium. The branching, stringlike tubes of a fungus, often underground. Mushrooms sprout from the mycelium.

nocturnal. Describes an animal that is active at night and rests during the day.

omnivore. An animal that eats both plants and meat.

ovipositor. The organ used by many female insects to lay eggs.

pioneer species. A plant or animal species that is among the first to grow in an area after a disturbance, such as fire.

protonema (plural protonemata). The rootlike threads that grow from the spore of a moss. After the protonema has a good hold on the ground, it grows buds that sprout into stalks of moss.

resin. A sticky secretion produced by conifers that does not dissolve in water. In serotinous cones, the resin hardens and holds the cone shut until melted by fire.

rhizome. A horizontal stem that grows underground, with roots reaching down and buds on top.

sclerotium. In some fungi, a clump of hardened tissue (made of mycelium) for storing food. It often forms during winter.

self-pruning. Said of trees whose lower branches die or fall off as the tree grows taller. This helps prevent fuel "ladders" that fire can travel on up to the treetops.

serotinous cone. A cone that needs fire to melt the resin holding the scales closed. When the scales open, the seeds inside fall out.

snag. A dead tree that remains standing.

species. A group of living things (plants, animals, fungi) with common characteristics; a subgroup of a genus. In scientific names, the second word of the name. For example, *albicaulis* is the species name of the whitebark pine, *Pinus albicaulis*.

spore. A microscopic, seedlike structure produced by mosses, fungi, and liverworts for reproduction. Spores are simpler than seeds and have only one parent.

stand-replacing fire. A very severe fire where all the trees burn, allowing new saplings to replace old trees. See **high-severity fire**.

surface fire. A fire that burns low plants and shrubs but does not reach up into the mature trees.

Index

adaptation, 1, 3, 18
Africa, 1
aspen, quaking, 28-29, 34, 48, 50
Australia, 1

bark, 8, 14, 18, 48, 49, 50
bear, grizzly, 24, 30, 38-39, 47, 48-49
beetle, 2, 3, 6, 30-31, 47; black fire, 8-9, 47; tunnels, 21,
    47; whitespotted sawyer, 42-43
berry, 30, 32, 33, 38, 47
blanketflower, 16-17, 48
bluebird: eastern, 4; mountain, 4, 36-37, 49; western, 4
borers, flat-headed, 47
bud, 18, 28, 32

cache/caching, 22
cambium, 14
camouflage, 16
Canada, 1
cavity nester, 36-37, 47
Ceanothus velutinus (snowbrush), 20-21, 50
Ceratodon purpureus (fire moss), 42-43, 48
Cervus canadensis (elk), 34-35, 48
chipmunk, 47, 48, 50
chlorophyll, 46
clone, 28, 50
cone: larch, 18; pine, 10, 14, 22-23, 24-25, 49; serotinous,
    10, 49
conifer, 18, 28, 38

deer, 47; mule, 48, 50
disturbance, 3
diurnal, 48
dormant, 20

egg, laying of, 6, 8, 26, 42, 48, 49
elk, 29, 34-35, 47, 48, 50; bugling, 48
Epilobium angustifolium (fireweed), 44-45, 48

fire: crown, 2; high-severity, 1, 2, 32, 49; low-severity,
    1, 20, 32; medium-severity, 18, 20, 32, 50; mixed-
    severity, 2, 34, 49; severe, 16, 40; stand-replacing, 2;
    surface, 1, 14, 18, 24, 32, 49, 50
fire moss, 42-43, 48
firemoth, Colorado, 16-17, 48
fireweed, 34, 44-45, 48
fungus, 12, 26, 28, 30, 49

Gaillardia aristata (blanketflower), 16-17, 48
gemma, 40
genus, 4

hibernate, 38
hormone, 28
huckleberry, 34, 38, 39; big, 32-33, 47
hummingbird, 45, 48

infrared radiation, 8
insect, 1, 8, 16, 17, 26, 27, 28, 42, 43, 48; as food, 6, 30,
    36, 38, 47

larch, western, 2, 18–19, 50
Larix occidentalis (western larch), 18–19, 50
larva, 6, 26, 36, 38, 47, 48, 49
liverwort, lung, 40–41, 49

Marchantia polymorpha (lung liverwort), 40–41, 49
Melanophila acuminata (black fire beetle), 8–9, 47
Morchella: angusticeps, conica, elata (black morel),
    12–13, 47
morel, black, 12–13, 38, 47
mosaic (landscape), 34
mouse, deer, 30–31, 38, 48, 50
mushroom, 1, 12–13, 38, 47
mycelium, 12

needle (tree), 10, 14, 18, 49
nocturnal, 30
North America, 1
Nucifraga columbiana (Clark's nutcracker), 22–23, 47
nut, 30
nutcracker, Clark's, 22–23, 24–25, 47, 50

omnivore, 30, 38
ovipositor, 26

Peromyscus maniculatus (deer mouse), 30–31, 48
Picoides arcticus (black-backed woodpecker), 6–7, 47
pine: lodgepole, 10–11, 30, 49, 50; ponderosa, 14–15, 49;
    whitebark, 22–23, 24–25, 38, 47, 50
Pinus: albicaulis, 24–25, 50; *contorta latifolia*, 10–11, 49;
    ponderosa, 14–15, 49
pioneer: plant, 42; species, 24, 48
pits, infrared-sensing, 8
Populus tremuloides (quaking aspen), 28–29, 50
predator, 36
protonema, 42

resin, 10, 49
rhizome, 32, 48
Rocky Mountains (Rockies), 1, 28, 48, 49, 50
roots, 20, 28, 32, 38, 50
Russia, 1

Schinia masoni (Colorado firemoth), 16–17, 48
scientific name, 4
sclerotium, 12
seed, 10, 14, 18, 20, 22, 24, 30, 38, 44, 47, 48, 49, 50
self-pruning, 14, 18
serotinous. *See* cone, serotinous
Sialia currucoides (mountain bluebird), 36–37, 49
Sirex species. *See* wasp, horntail
snag, 34, 47
snowbrush, 20–21, 30, 34, 50
South America, 1
species, 3, 4, 48, 49
spore, 26, 40, 42, 47, 48, 49
squirrel, 24, 47; ground, 38

tunnel. *See* beetle; wasp, horntail

United States, 1
Urocerus species. *See* wasp, horntail
Ursus arctos horribilis (grizzly bear), 38–39, 48–49

Vaccinium membranaceum (big huckleberry), 32–33, 47

wasp, horntail, 26–27, 49; tunnel, 26
woodpecker, 36; black-backed, 6–7, 47

About the Author & Illustrator

Beth A. Peluso has been drawing and writing since she could hold a pencil. She has a BA in writing with a minor in studio art from Augustana College in Illinois. Her MS in Environmental Studies from the University of Montana in Missoula allowed her to combine her interests in writing, art, and the natural world. The journal *The Prairie Naturalist* selected one of her watercolors for its annual cover.

Beth is an avid birder and spent two summers doing field research in Arizona and the Sierra Nevada in California. She regularly leads local Audubon walks and participates in volunteer owl surveys. She's survived being a day camp counselor and substitute teacher, and has been teaching fencing (yes, the kind with swords) for four years. While living in Montana, she became fascinated with the role of fire in the forests, especially after tromping around burn sites and discovering lush fields of fireweed and great birding. She currently lives in Juneau, Alaska, where she's learning about ocean tides and a rain forest too soggy to burn. *The Charcoal Forest* is her first book.

—Lauren Oakes photo

Mountain Press Books for Young Readers

_____	Awesome Ospreys: *Fishing Birds of the World*, AGES 8 AND UP	$12.00
_____	The Charcoal Forest: *How Fire Helps Animals and Plants*, AGES 8 AND UP	$12.00
_____	Loons: *Diving Birds of the North*, AGES 8 AND UP	$12.00
_____	Nature's Yucky!: *Gross Stuff That Helps Nature Work*, AGES 5 AND UP	$10.00
_____	Nature's Yucky! 2: *The Desert Southwest*, AGES 5 AND UP	$12.00
_____	Owls: *Whoo are they?*, AGES 8 AND UP	$12.00
_____	Sacagawea's Son: *The Life of Jean Baptiste Charbonneau*, AGES 10 AND UP	$10.00
_____	Spotted Bear: *A Rocky Mountain Folktale*, AGES 5 AND UP	$15.00
_____	Stories of Young Pioneers: *In Their Own Words*, AGES 10 AND UP	$14.00

Please include $3.00 shipping and handling for 1–4 books and $5.00 for 5 or more books.

Send the books marked above. I have enclosed $_____

Name _____ Phone_____

Address _____

City / State / Zip _____

☐ Payment enclosed (check or money order in U.S. funds)

Bill my: ☐ VISA   ☐ Mastercard   ☐ American Express   ☐ Discover

Card No. _____ Expiration Date_____

Signature _____

MOUNTAIN PRESS PUBLISHING COMPANY
P.O. Box 2399 • Missoula, Montana 59806
406-728-1900 • fax 406-728-1635 • toll-free 800-234-5308
info@mtnpress.com • www.mountain-press.com